John Siddique'
The Prize was publ.
appeared in numerous anthologies and magazines in the
UK and abroad, and he has held many commissions and
residencies including Ilkley Literature Festival, Ledbury
Poetry Festival, HMYOI Wetherby, Rainer, Commonword
and BBC Manchester. He teaches and mentors creative
writing for many institutions including The Arvon
Foundation.

More information at: **www.johnsiddique.co.uk**

Poems from a Northern Soul

John Siddique

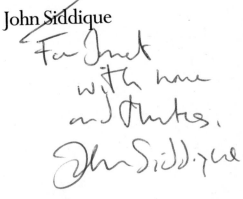

For Janet
with love
and thanks.
John Siddique

Poems from a Northern Soul
Published 2007 by Crocus

Crocus Books are published by
Commonword Ltd
6 Mount Street
Manchester
M2 5NS

Printed by LPPS

British Library Cataloguing-In-Publications Data:
A cataloguing record for this book is available from the
British Library.

For my family wherever I may find them

Contents

Visible Imprints
Desire for Sight (after Lorca)   11
Visible Imprints   12
To the Iron Waters   13
Every Day   15
A Map of Rochdale   16
What is the night full of when it is empty?   17
Blue   18
Julie   19
A Big Mac and Two Happy Meals   20
The Morning Train   21
There in the Song   22
Moonbow   23
To the Leader of the Free World   24
Reality Programming, Falinge   25
Finding an Edge   26
Dark Valley   27
Both Hungry   28
Mother's Day   29
Above Eye Level   30

Available Light
The Double   35
Two Meanings   36
Radiance   37
Discord   38

Great Ancoats Street   39
Dogs – Salford   42
Chorltonville   43
Industrial Landscape   44

Northern Soul

A Housing Interview   47
Kathy   48
Posters on the Walls at Alcohol Drug Services   49
One of Three Jims   50
Sheltered Accommodation   51
Plans   53
Youth Court Waiting Area   54
Trying to Get Me   55
Veronica   56
Blessing   57
Inner view   58
Levi   60
The Young Gods   61
King Street, Wigan   62

Visible Imprints

Desire for Sight (after Lorca)

When gossip starts all that is left is gossip.

When fear takes hold, all that is left is the fear.

Fold away your papers,
colour in the outlines.

Regret is the first town our train will pass though.

Unknowing, the confusion of unknowing.

Let my country see itself,
may its people be visible to each other.

Visible Imprints

Love burns his diaries in the zinc leaf bin
in the garden. Sick of himself, he's a fool
who gets it wrong, turns up in a pink wig
and sequins to a dinner party, thinking
it's fancy dress. Cries when he says *I love you,*
when he only meant to say *pass the salt.*
He would like to unfold the paper of his heart,
give you the pen to write your lines there.

Anniversaries and Christmases make him sad.
Young love is so self obsessed, middle love sees
what you mean, though you have no intention
of saying it. He's learned that turning up
on time, doing what you say you're going to do,
allowing two to remain two, are the answers.
His head full of Hollywood, full of perfect wives
in the aisles of Tescos, the escalators at Brixton tube.

His heart decides forgiveness means peace,
means letting go of the grasping. He gathers
kindling, the red petrol canister from the boot
of the car, burns the diaries full of their names.
Gives up on longing at his core, in that way
he can have you again. No more pushing away.
Red edged burning, ash paper with imprints
still visible, fireflies of years — messages on the air,
caught down-drafted into wet. He can go to bed
tonight, put his arms round his girl; be there finally.

To the Iron Waters

From our house at Regent Street,
out from the family firing line,
by passing each netted window,
a street full of Catholics.
The red phone box by the junk-yard
in the distance, a first marker.
Then the anarchist A in a circle
sprayed onto the wall one night in 1977
in a hopeful pink enamel.

Folly Walk where I sometimes talk
to the tramp who makes the bench there
his morning checkpoint,
Red-Stripe in his hand.
It settles the nerves, he says.

Opening out,
Cronkeyshaw Common.
The bus stop at Syke Common where
we hang in the evening, each one of us
is in love with Anna Duffy, she only
goes out with lads with cars.

Into the green,
tracking the pubs,
The Donkey, The Hunter's Rest.
A private fishing lodge where Kevin Isaac
shot birds, and I cried at their small limpness.

To the Iron Waters,
freezing over red stones.
A mouthful for a tonic. Bathing
your feet for waking up and forgetting.

Every Day

Trying to leave. The front door already
closed. Back in to see if the gas is off.
Halfway down the street, go back to see
if you locked the door. Then from the train
ringing your neighbour who has the key
to ask her to check the iron is switched off.

Trying to allow time to check these things.
Trying to make a list to undo the forgetfulness,
but in the effort, leaving the almost empty
kettle on the hob in the bright sunlight,
you can't see the flame. Come back home
to a house full of smoke, a bottomless chunk
of hot metal.

Leaving lists on the mirror, just short of swearing
at yourself, leave loving notes the book says.
Leaving time to check everything. Leaving earlier
than you need to, you find yourself twiddling
forgotten thumbs on the station platform.

A Map of Rochdale

We are not London or Germany.
The war barely touched us here. I am drained
by allusions and distances, signs to twin towns
hundreds of miles away, replicas of clock towers,
the clone shop confusion of every town high street.

Let us make our own map of the sprawl,
its life and ours, a bit unseemly and tough,
filled with early sexual adventures
stemming from boredom and flesh. Politics
grown from isolation and inverted snobbery.

We'll rename the streets after their real stories,
Smack Head Valley. Skinhead Avenue,
Race Riot Street. Touch Me There Road.
Drug Deal Walk. First Kiss Gardens.
Pissed-up Lane. Possibility Fields.

What is the night full of when it is empty?

The closed curtains protect him, inside a man
is dancing to the radio: a seven year old boy,
flapping his shoulders like wings. Pulsing
his belly like a worm. The sky is clear outside.
A three quarter moon headlight.
Upstairs they're stomping around causing
his windows to rattle in their frames. They murmur,
as if they've been drinking. Stopping his dance,
turning the radio off, no clear words. Listening
to the stories in their muffled voices.

Blue

It was blue. The sort of blue that makes you
want to steal cars. The sort of blue that has you
pedal to the metal, sirens behind you,
face puffed with blood. Temples and hands tight.

It was the sort of blue that makes you
have to hide your stiffy with a shopping bag,
so you can get off the bus. The sort of blue
to turn my guts to a washing machine on cycle A.

Just a T-Shirt. But how she wears it,
as if she's a present that needs unwrapping.

Julie

I lost my friend Dave over Julie Connell.
She was longhaired, black Irish, all the allure
of a Spanish invader. We drank vodka and kissed,
I swear it was after she'd left him.

She copied me *The Lamb Lies Down on Broadway*
by Genesis onto a green Sony tape, which I played
everyday, trying to fathom meaning in its poetry.

Julie left me for a biker after six months or so.
I listened to her tape even more for a while,
full of big tears, until I loved it more than her.

I saw them one night in our pub, walked out
and never went back. Dave and I tried to be
friends again, some broken things won't fix.
He told me he'd seen her, she was living near
her parents, she'd had a boy and a girl,
the biker had left her for a drug habit.

Last year I found myself driving past where
I thought she lived. I remembered her breasts,
she had the faintest down of light hair between
them, where I would kiss the salt.

A Big Mac and Two Happy Meals

McDonald's Saturday morning, the men
have shields of steel under their coats.
A reality family drama: ten a.m. any Saturday
you like, sit with your coffee, watch the time
reflected in the plate window.

It shouldn't be like this, his story goes,
they should be in a heap on the settee watching
Scooby Doo.

At these bleach-wiped melamine tables,
the exchange of words: a setting of limits
at the sharp edge of family.

The Morning Train

No-one holds hands. No-one is kissing
No-one is shaking hands.

A group of six men talking three different languages.

A tall man in bad shoes reading his paper, secretly
looks at everyone. He's sat next to a large sleeping
black woman who pulls her legs under her
like a nesting chicken, he gives her the look,
scanning her like he is some human photocopier,
then moves further down the carriage to escape his fear.

There in the Song

Loan shark, foreclosing on our life.
Broken chord of dreams, of a life in the light.

I see your promises waiting around every corner.
When I get there you're gone, were never there.

Down down, deeper and down
The world becomes small, a vest that's shrunk

in the wash, or have I slipped on a few pounds
waiting for the insured promises to mature.

The radio saves my life, all that small talk,
I tell the dj to shut the fuck up as I'm driving.

Somehow the noise is better than looking back at
all the *should have beens*. I see chimneys fall,

buildings collapse, we lose our dreams at some point,
a pickpocket, or a burglar, an unfaithful friend.

The radio saves my mind, a line from a song
that makes sense in a way that you can't explain.

I can take it all from you. Again, again, again, again.
Not yet but soon, again, I'll make better promises.

Moonbow

We saw a moonbow arc the night.

We saw a moonbow stand from hill to hill.

A light distant rain refracts,
throwing night colours,
pots of silver at each end.

One day we fold our arms in.
One day we fold our arms in.

The banshee cuts our feet and legs.
One day we fold our arms in.

Stop running to find silver,
chasing single moon-bowed thought.

She is the night herself.

To the Leader of the Free World

Your empire will go the way of all empires.
Your outlets will become wild gardens.
Your motorways, migration paths for buffalo.
Maize will be sown in the dust you have left.

In New York harbour, two broken metal legs,
on the pedestal, these words, *Give me your tired,*
your poor, your huddled masses yearning
to breath free. We will come to this new land,
never knowing your philosophy, that
an empire begins with an open hand.

Reality Programming, Falinge

There are no stagehands, no band.
The actors are out having supper.
There are only the voices of the cleaners,
chatting and rising as they pick up papers,
mint flavoured silver foil, ticket stubs,
the odd dropped coin. This amphitheatre,
a coliseum of resourcefulness.
Solving the fifties' baby boom/housing crisis
through theatre. New homes for old. Build to the sky.
People moved like pieces in a game of draughts,
whilst being told they're in a game of chess.

It's a where you were born thing. A who you know thing.
Your hourly mantra, *Do you want a cup of tea?*
You keep the kitchen light off to observe
the play below. The endless taxis
for the people downstairs. *It's better now,*
they've put the cameras in, safer.
Up the lamppost-high watchtowers, galvanised
against the weather, painted with anti-graffiti,
no climb paint. The poles wear a necklace of spikes
to protect the black ball of the eye. We dream
of being famous for something on tv.

Finding an Edge

Where is there an edge?
At the end of the forest?
Staring at the sea? It rolls,
pulls back thin, clear green,
grinds the rock, moves tons
of sand, throws out plastic bottles.
Leaves me unchanged, still whole,
when I want to be torn apart.

Dark Valley

The train takes a long time to come out
of the Calder Valley, mile after mile
of vaginal darkness, clamping her men tight.

Her down of trees waits to bud and plume
back after Bridgit's day. We wash the grime
of wintering from our faces, lay plans down,
feel the quickening that makes this journey
out, a gathering into self.

I stand alone on the hill, a tree grows up
behind me, the father tree,
away a little from him, the grandfather.

The valley walls are high and dark. Stone furrows
ploughed by huge boulders once held
in the hands of a forgotten glacier.

And the world opens out. Flat farm land
of an old feudal kingdom. The dry stone walls
have moved, we never seem to stray far
or break them down for too long.

Borders change but she still holds us.
Men clutching after mother-love. Keeping
ourselves and our minds hard to please her.

Both Hungry

Angry and Silent.
A two headed horse

cannot decide who will eat
the only flower left
in the red field.

Mother's Day

The mother you are determines what your
child will become.

The child you are determines what kind of
mother you will grow to be.

And most of what you'll do, you'll never be thanked for.

This is the circle for mothers, who turn the world
with their hands while no one is watching.

Above Eye Level

He walks to the station, pockets the tickets
of a cheap day return with one hand,
clicks the keys of his phone with the thumb
of the other. Makes his entry onto platform,
which hollows with announcements.

He likes to make entrances in everyday places
that don't expect him. His brown pinstripe suit
cuts the morning air. The air thickens with light,
soft as milky coffee, he wants to drink it down
by the glassful, or pour himself into it.
He wants to sit and not exist separately from this,
the station cat seeking attention around his legs.

Boarding the two-carriage train facing
the direction of movement, a surprise
meeting catches him: the odour
of tumble-dried clothing mixing with
the scent of a man who believes he is
too busy to bathe. They are old friends,
one sharp, the other older. Older keeps on
moving on, made his money by saving
every penny, recycling food, renting out property.
They have their usual run of conversation,
both present but not present. The morning air
asking for silence, a silence that is not possible.
It waits outside of time while we have our ideas
of ourselves. Leaving layers of hills and chimneys

they pass through northern towns and upon reaching
the city they part in a friendly manner.
It's been a long time since they talked.

Above the brickwork of department stores,
electrical shops, there are high up places
where he doesn't often look. Sandstone opens
its mouth, tries to tell him something. Red brick
becomes a mirror. Above the facades
of shop frontages the architecture of personality
remains. He stands in this city, puts on his headphones,
doesn't press play. There is a word waiting:
a noun dressed in the clothes of a verb,
busy doing and being. He looks above the shop fronts,
the blinded windows of luxury apartments,
the dirty windows of words.

Available Light

The Double

It takes a long time
to feel beautiful,
then when you are old enough
to be confident it has
gone.

Two Meanings

Loose hair marks the nubile state.

Bound,
she is married.

Radiance

At seven a.m. when nothing can be bought,
the items in the shop window exist
for their own sakes. Each thing in time will belong
to someone. Go from here into the world,
a gift or a treat, as a token of love or a peace offering.

Traffic files past, desires get stirred, expressions
of self, decorations for home. There is so much
expectation at seven a.m. when the sun hits
the wooden panelling charging it with life,
the cash till keeps its mouth shut.

Discord

Mum won't look at me,
she is frozen in her staring away.
I don't know what to say or do
I have my coat on to leave.

My sister tries to push a reaction.
The little ones move noisily,
creating more pain
in the aching kitchen.

Great Ancoats Street

Boy on the corner waiting for his Da
to come out of the pub.

Ever since you put me here there has only
been silence. Ever since you put me here
day and night locked, time passed me by.

Boy on the corner stood here in snow, then
stood here in sun. Ever since you put me here
in a game of hide and seek that never ends.

Ever since you put me here at twilight
for a last gleaming of possible futures.

Boy on the corner, has less life here than
the warehouses at his back.

Boy on the corner, skinny legs can't do much.

Ever since you put me here, there has been
constant change. Ever since you put me here
it has always been the same.

Coins in his pocket. Rehearsed words in his head
to get his dad home. Familiar cap pulls him up
in his head. Cold knees. Pants a bit tight. Cracked
leather shoe. Little man's jacket pulling slightly
under the armpits.

The clearest thing in this half-lit, half made up
place are the banisters and street lamps.

Since you put me here you have imagined
the world of my eyes. Ever since you put me here
you see yourself as the boy on the corner.
Ever since you put me here you think you are me.

This is just a somewhere people pass through,
not a place to stand forever.

Bed shops, metal workers, cafés, the great
smoking damp mill. The canal, the barges
away down the street.

Boy on the corner. Self-awareness extremed
in pencil lines. Lostlings – we wait and wait.

The road will get wider, the print works will print
papers for a few years, then the windows become
target practice for stone throwers.

Boy on the corner, becomes old man.
There will still be the bed shops, canal and mill
and a boy on the corner.

Housing estate and industrial estate
backing onto each other. There is little to do
but stand on the corner. Think about playing
chicken across the road.

Go down to the canal.

Pull faces at the condoms.

Throw stones.

Dogs – Salford

The family dog has had enough of their talking
he sits by the red lamppost, dreams dog wishes.

The stray dog plays with two girls for a while
they throw for her, give her a sweet.

Two dogs: best friends all their lives,
out for a walk, waiting for each other

as they piss on and scent each lamppost
of their street in turn.

This is a time when our doors were open
when we shared our lives on the street.

Grey dog sits among the strollers. Kids in
red and blue pass him by.

Grey dog watches them all pass. The lady
at the black door comes out for the first time

in days. A nun is busy on Jesus' business.
Jimbo with beard talks from an upstairs window.

Chorltonville

We walk in night air.
A perfect ellipse of the estate.

Drawn to windows,
lit rooms,
life in each cell.

Try to see the books on the bookshelf.
Wish I could see what you're eating.

In each cell:
containment,
and the rudder.

Some rooms open
so easily, it causes envy
as the light bulbs show this world.

Different from our own world.

Fixed and square,
these rooms are the ships
that hold us.

Industrial Landscape

She stands reflecting herself in the placement
of chimneys. Hill of ash black.
Oldham smokes distance.

Lead me through streets, funnelling,

past a funeral. Black hat.
Black horses. No flowers.
Blocking the airway to whited-out Pennines.

Babies in prams, dogs and back yards, oblivious
as the porcelain heads mid-ground to reclamations
at the Catholic church.

Her mind rises with the gasometers,
over ship canal and dock, over Strangeways
and Manchester, rising on thermals of industry.

Northern Soul

A Housing Interview

Who's your housing aid officer?
Is it the decision you're waiting for?
You're just waiting to hear?
I'll make a note of that.

You're in the 'Quality' Hotel now?
Have you been moving about quite a lot?
Everyone like you is moving around a lot.

Other options – Speak to Dave.

What are the special circumstances?
Have you had a homeless decision yet?
If you have had a 193 decision you can
bid for properties. If you have any questions…

Have you provided proof of identity?
I'll just need to speak to housing benefit.
I just need you to sign this.

Note: A 193 means you are officially homeless in Wigan

Kathy

She holds her own hand softly.
Touches her face when she talks.

Moves her left leg in anticipation
of herself — a little fountain of speech
bubbling over each thing that she loves.

Going to the Café Nirvana tonight
into the mosh pit to be herself.

There's a dream of a Sunday dinner waiting
for her either at the sheltered accommodation,
or in a flat in Hindley, Ince or Leigh.

Eighteen in three months, her birthday is Halloween,
dressing up for both, a trick or a treat.

Posters on the Walls at Alcohol Drug Services

We are always striving
to improve the quality of our services.

Transcendental meditation.
I ♥ Life.
Sexual Abuse!

Regrets I've had a few.
Keep your medication safe.
Are you responsible?
Drop in and share.

I remember this one time
I did a bit with two other people.

Free information and guidance.
Free confidential sex advice.
Looking for a brighter future?
Depression can be beaten.

One of Three Jims

There is a space there where James used to be.
I have never met him before and I'm not meeting
him now. So much violence in his world,

he's an insecure house on a rainy Wigan day.
There is a space there above the jaw, below
the forehead. He's a blue track-suited shadow,
a white-trainered smiling geezer.

So much, too much in his world. He's a quiet smile
in a vacuum filled with noise.

Sheltered Accommodation

I

You could strike a match on the industrial blue
carpet that leads you round these corridors
of hope. The inhabitants don't call it hope,
but they're all waiting for someone or something
in their self-storage unit flats where they have
put themselves as a last and first resort.

The chip fat and fags cling to the yellow walls.
How old is the oil? How many cigarettes?
Each meal and smoke is a tick on faces
of these young clocks.

II

Blue steel pillars hold the mill conversion
at regular intervals.
If these pillars were trees they would have doves
in their branches. These trees of life holding my roof up.
Counting the pillars on my corridor.
1. The tree of life.
2. The tree of knowledge.
3. The tree of death.
4. The tree of wishes.
5. The tree of fire.

I am a pillar of smoke, the pillar of life,
I am the roots, I am the branches.
Pillar, door. Pillar, door, leading to sunlit windows.
Looking over Uncle Joe's Mint Ball factory, the railway line,
the BT building pretending to be a 1960's comprehensive.
Is that Parbold in the distance? And Preston beyond that?

Plans

Plans blow apart.
Work falls to bits,
and we spin conversation,
and file paperwork,
make new plans, arrangements
for tomorrow. *Be there at ten.*
always playing it by ear.

Youth Court Waiting Area

A five year old dances around
the coke machine. The air is church clear,
air conditioned, and the pews are
as uncomfortable on the sitting bones.
So we lean, stand, rattle the change
in our pockets, fiddle with keys,
eye a young copper.

What prayers lie under the waiting?
These people don't come with sub-titles,
but the truth is carved in the table top
in blue biro, *Dumbo 2005 — Hi as a kite,*
Michelle was here, so was Tony,
Karen and a hundred others,
the table is mostly covered
with tags. A record of the time
spent waiting to find out about
how time will be spent.

The policeman is younger than us,
so we must be getting old.
The lawyers are here more than those
waiting, a purgatory, a prison;
compensated by legal aid wage packets,
and lots of holidays.

Hands in pockets, hands over mouths,
fingers text and check phones, gum is clicked
in mouths as bored as brick walls.

Trying to Get Me

I talk with my mouth closed.
Look with my head down,
see with my eyes shut, always
checking my reflection.

I listen through my own agenda.
Talk with the voices of the child
I used to be, appealing, mewling
to the parent in you.

I sit here while you sort my life out.
I'll eat my ice cream while you rack
your brains. I'm getting away with it,
while the papers and files pile up.

Veronica

The windows don't work in the court,
and the ones that do don't show anything.

Wigan is a grey slur in August.
Veronica shakes her leg moving the whole bench.

The whole family are here; it's no day out,
waiting in the café over tea that's only been
shown the bag, over bacon butties to keep them going.
She holds herself up with stories of how. Emphatic
pokes at the table. Her wide legs taking
it all in, tagging and curfewing her experience.

She talks but she's listening, learning circuits,
she doesn't get it yet, but the accumulation
is coming, the time is coming. It's all down
to her to stop being the only girl who

Blessing

When you walk,
I will walk with you.

When you cry,
I will cry too.

We are bound together
in some way.

It hurts
and it's good.

Innerview

Donna asks the questions.
Gemma folds her arms.

The questions are long,
her answers are short.

As the interview goes on
she begins to gesticulate

demonstrating time in blocks,
thought moving through her fingers.

They talk in profile, trying
to clear up the circumstances,

what help she might need.
Her living situation, she wants to move.

Needs a little help with moving flat.
She gets a bit confused.

Donna and Gemma become mirrors,
both flick their feet,

both cross their legs in the same direction.
Sifting the info, fixing a picture

beginning to identify a way.
Explaining the confidential aspects.

Gemma's building herself back up
after the passing of her gran.

Brave enough to say that she needs
help with this and that.

Singing her heart out to a karaoke
machine in her flat, on her own.

She closes the door, closes her eyes
and dances in her music by herself.

Levi

There's a certainty under the skin,
a kind of dance that wants to manifest
itself in stillness. He's riding his own wave,

making a circle about himself, drawing
a pond of cold water under morning light.

Levi has learned to take a place in the world.
Lifted himself out of drinking and disorder.
Now he wants to break his circumference,
cease to be a circle, unjoin his hands.

The Young Gods

The young gods sit, boxers ready for the ring.
Boys with meaty hands, defending themselves,
arms starting to cut into musculature.

Warren is full of sunlight, he soaks it in everyday,
working outside. He is a compass checking directions.
Facing West he pieces his day together moving
from sleeping couch to work, no fixed abode.
He's a clear line, it's his ethic that keeps him clean,
walking his way to some kind of space.

Sean is moon pale, works the same landscape
as Warren. The sun has not caught Sean yet.
He doesn't like to talk too much, mustn't give himself away.
He's a young boy and a teenager at the same time.
Eight year old Sean looks out of nineteen year old eyes,
both of himselves awkward and proud.

Young fighters, young gods of the clubs, the streets.
Quiet before action. The world is on probation with them.
Quiet after their fights, taking each thump into their bodies.
Soaking up the shocks which they say don't bother them,
wearing them in their faces. They're cutting lines,
        keeping light.

King Street, Wigan

Behind the theme bar facades is a town.
Behind the attitudes there's Saturday night.
Behind Saturday night is the shadow of the week.
We make ourselves all week.
Blow it all down on King Street, where the fighting
has turned to *destroy at all costs,* where the flirting
has a slap down waiting in it. The Saturday night grab,
drunk and fucking our northern souls away,
if we're lucky. Or shouting the tribal *Oi!*
With hot sauce on our kebabs if we're not.

Acknowledgements

My thanks and love to the following people who make being a poet worth the while: Hannah Nunn, Euan & Ffion Atkinson, Simon & Rose Howarth, Kath Siddique, Chris Robinson, Stephen Hughes, John Holland, Xanthe Gresham, Sherry Robinson, Mel Abrahams, Nadia Gilani, Rosie Garland, Cherry Smyth, Adrian Fox, Adam Fieled, Gary Mckeone, Mike and Dean at The Rialto, Helen Robinson, Tom Palmer, Ray French, James Nash, Ian & Isabel at ROUTE, Brothatalk, Cathy & Pete at Commonword.

Thanks to Commonword, BBC Manchester, Rainer Wigan, and The Lowry for commissioning these poems from me over the years, and thanks to Mark Doty for inspiring the poem *Above eye level*.

'Half of man is his tongue, and the other half is his heart: the rest is only an image composed of blood and flesh.' - Zuhyar ibn Abu Sulma (6th century C.E.)

Lots of love

John Siddique

Also by the same author:

Poetry:
The Devil's Lunchbox (Mongrel Press)
The Prize (Rialto)
Transparency (as Editor, Crocus)

For Children:
*Don't wear it on your head,
don't stick it down your pants*
(Inscribe/Peepal Tree)

Prose:
Four Fathers (Co-author, Route)

Some of the poems in this collection have appeared in
the following magazines and anthologies:
Visible Imprints, *Both Hungry* and *There in the Song*
— BBC Manchester website
Industrial Landscape — Rain Dog
Julie — Smiths Knoll
Blue — Brothatalk
Two Meanings — Hair (Suitcase).
Mother's Day is from the play AND SHE WAS